Sound of anklets

Kashinath Karmakar

Sanjuktaa Asopa

Art by Sankara Sudanagunta

ISBN 979-8-89277-315-7

Dedications

For my mother and my wife---kash poet

For my parents who never left---sanjuktaa

Acknowledgement

All the poems in this collection have been published before in various haiku journals like The Heron's Nest, Frogpond, Modern Haiku, Tinywords, Cattails, A Hundred Gourds,haikuKATHA, Muse India and Daily haiku, to name a few and been placed in various contests. Our heartfelt thanks to all these editors. We are grateful to Anitha Verma who helped us with the selection of poems in the initial stages and of course, Kala Ramesh, for her guidance and for writing the introduction to our book. And our special thanks to Sankara Sudanagunta, the young haiku poet, who agreed to provide the art to adorn our humble collection.

A deep bow to you all,
Kash & sanjuktaa

Foreword

Sound of Anklets, by Kashinath Karmarkar and Sanjuktaa Asopa, offers a blend of originality and good control over technique, and the result is a masterpiece.

deafening rain / to think it has no sound / of its own

There are a few haiku you like on your first read and which do not disappoint in subsequent readings, either. This haiku of Kashinath's is one such poem for me. There is a controlled release of emotions in most of his poems, a nuance that's difficult to capture.

opening the window / to a moth /and what's left of the moon

Sanjuktaa's poems are elusive and, like gently guarded secrets, reveal only a little to the reader at first glance. What I love most about her poems is the 'soft landing' she achieves in each line.

The interleaving of two distinctive poetic voices is highly effective. Brevity releases language as darkness releases a star! Get your copy today and you will be well rewarded.

– Kala Ramesh

Page 1

First trimester-
her new password
a baby's name

morning glory-
for a moment
I am the butterfly

– Kashinath

Page 2

Sunday morning-
helping a wisteria
To stand again

sound of rain-
i fold her last love letter
into a paper boat

– Kashinath

Page 3

breakfast table
the light
from a peeled orange

I, too
woke up late—
wild violets

– sanjuktaa

Page 4

roadside inn
the scent of sunlight
in leaf cups

forgotten frost
I add a name back
to my contacts

– sanjuktaa

Page 5

half bloomed rose
an ant enters into
its fragrance

meditation hour-
sound of someone's broom
clearing trash

– kashinath

Page 6

hula hooping-
a gypsy girl's hips
sway my mind

rose garden-
I tuck another dream
into her hair

– kashinath

Page 7

dreaming the sky ...
a broken swing sunk
in the bluebells

shallows...
sunlight the shape
of koi

– sanjuktaa

Page 8

meditation mat
I check for
the invisible ants

on the fence
morning glories
and my opinion

– sanjuktaa

Page 9

sudden breeze-
my every pansy
a butterfly

waking me up
from my midnight dream-
glass bangles

– kashinath

Page 10

traffic jam-
trimming a haiku
to fit the syllables

this vagabond life-
symmetry in the wings
of a butterfly

– kashinath

opening the window
to a moth
and what's left of the moon

– sanjuktaa

Page 12

after all the things
that have gone wrong
plum blossoms

spring shadows-
new razor
for the teenaged son

– sanjuktaa

spring fever-
in the parking lot her cycle
rests on mine

– kashinath

Page 14

stranded
where her neckline takes a dip-
a blue vein

a whiff of jasmine
as she unties her hair-
hint of rain

– kashinath

Page 15

spring rain
the depth
of
a tulip

stars
not wished upon
… now that the dandelions

– sanjuktaa

Page 16

dry well
I haul up a bucket
filled with summer

the faint curve
of a bare shoulder ...
tropical night

– sanjuktaa

Page 17

air hostess-
her eyeliner's tail pointing
towards the sky

adding wings
to our eyelashes-
butterfly kiss

– kashinath

Page 18

cloudy day-
all the sunflowers facing
each other

old sycamore-
the heart between our names
larger now

                                              – kashinath

Page 19

this puddle
what my paper boat knows
of the sea

– sanjuktaa

Page 20

back to school
unlearning
the whole summer

roadside bistro
a shot glass
full of rain

— sanjuktaa

Page 21

after the rain
in each hanging droplet
the world upside down

                                   – kashinath

pattern of her
fingertips on my bare back-
midnight rain

Father's Day-
in her sleep my wife
calls me dad

– kashinath

Page 23

simmering rice grains
in the pot—
patter of rain

sound of anklets
on the winding path ...
riversong

– sanjuktaa

Page 24

the long whistle
of the express train
I uncurl my toes

ginko walk
the teacher chatters on
about silence

– sanjuktaa

$\mathcal{P}$age 25

deafening rain-
to think it has no sound
of its own

– kashinath

monsoon sky-
from someone's guitar
Come September

monsoon lull-
the street dog in search
of a dry spot

– kashinath

Page 27

rocking chair
back and forth
between now and then

– sanjuktaa

Page 28

dewdrop ...
what does the leaf know
of nothingness

lace doilies ...
a spider crochets
the mist

– sanjuktaa

Page 29

autumn sky—
swaying wheat field
shaping the wind

windstorm-
all the dandelions
leave me behind

– kashinath

Page 30

window moon
an imperfect circle
in a perfect square

– kashinath

Page 31

galaxy …
just a lily-pond
will do

– sanjuktaa

Page 32

wheat ears—
the sunlight braided
by wind

walking the dog
a bit of meadow
between his teeth

– sanjuktaa

Page 33

evening mist-
a drunk man stops me to
ask the way to the moon

tipsy night-
chasing the moon
puddle after puddle

– kashinath

driftwood-
someday again
another shoreline

starlit night-
the distinct texture
of a fresh grave

– kashinath

Page 35

in an empty cicada shell
 the beginning of dusk

evening sea
the ferryman's call
almost blue
almost mist

– sanjuktaa

Page 36

October rain
the old umbrella
fails to open

paper boat
big enough to hold
a dream or two

– sanjuktaa

Page 37

after lovemaking
capturing the window moon
with every smoke ring

a big catch-
in the spider's web
the full moon

– kashinath

Page 38

kite festival-
yet another reason to look
at the sky

harvest song-
moonlight fills the beggar's
empty bowl

– kashinath

doomed
to sleepless nights ...
hare on the moon

crow feather—
before dusk
the feel of dusk

– sanjuktaa

reddening leaf ...
how the end
begins

scars
that have begun to heal—
purple asters

– sanjuktaa

Page 41

scar-
therefore
I am

– kashinath

Page 42

divorce decree-
sound of a chainsaw
cutting through a tree

what is left
and what was there-
crescent moon

– kashinath

Page 43

black water pond
how deep
the crow's eyes

taking
the blue notes higher
twilight gulls

– sanjuktaa

Page 44

low battery—
I hold on to her fading voice
a while longer

one part dusk
three parts loneliness ...
cricket calls

– sanjuktaa

Page 45

Marina beach-
waves go back
without touching your name

so much to say
and you're gone-
twilight sky

– kashinath

Page 46

butcher's shop-
the tremble of the goat
before and after

ghost town-
sound of army boots
from alley to alley

– kashinath

hush beyond the gunfire olive blossoms

desert night
the scent of campfire
in the dying stars

– sanjuktaa

Page 48

Milky way ...
a billion reasons
to love him

the slow drift
of an owl's feather
... stretching moonlight

–sanjuktaa

the silence
of the harvested field-
moonless night

winter again-
somehow a coriander leaf
inside my wallet

– kashinath

Page 50

first winter days-
again in Mom's frail hands
my unfinished sweater

faded album-
all the missing colors
of my childhood

– kashinath

Page 51

deep fog—
the streetlight floats
in an amniotic sac

riding down the escalator
scent of snow
on damp coats

– sanjuktaa

Page 52

winter night—
I dream
in monochrome

patches of snow
missed appointment
with the hair-colorist

– sanjuktaa

Page 53

first love-
I scold my dog for
chasing her cat

– kashinath

Page 54

cold wave-
the newsreader's sneeze
goes uncut

year's end-
only the sound of mouse clicks
from every desk

– kashinath

Page 55

shelling peas—
each passing year
like the one before

calm water—
a duck glides over
the morning star

– sanjuktaa

Page 56

fingernail moon
we share what's left
of the apple pie

– sanjuktaa

Page 57

crescent moon-
somewhere in the dark part
my shadow

home alone-
she talks to the baby
in her womb

– kashinath

paper boat-
how far it will carry
my child's smile

– kashinath

the last poem
signed with a flourish—
falling star

        – sanjuktaa